Ways to Be a
Hero

Charlotte Guillain

Raintree

www.raintreepublishers.co.uk
Visit our website to find out
more information about
Raintree books.

To order:
☎ Phone 0845 6044371
🖨 Fax +44 (0) 1865 312263
✉ Email myorders@raintreepublishers.co.uk

Customers from outside the UK please telephone +44 1865 312262

Edited by Andrew Farrow and Vaarunika Dharmapala
Designed by Richard Parker
Picture research by Ruth Blair
Originated by Capstone Global Library Ltd
Printed and bound in China by South China Printing
  Company Ltd

ISBN 978 1 406 21748 3 (hardback)
15 14 13 12 11
10 9 8 7 6 5 4 3 2 1

ISBN 978 1 406 21776 6 (paperback)
16 15 14 13 12
10 9 8 7 6 5 4 3 2 1

British Library Cataloguing in Publication Data
Guillain, Charlotte.
101 ways to be a hero.
158-dc22
A full catalogue record for this book is available
from the British Library.

Acknowledgments
We would like to thank the following for permission
to reproduce photographs: Corbis pp 13 (Andersen
Ross/Blend Images), 20 (Aude Guerrucci/Pool), 27
(Jack Hollingsworth), 29 (Poppy Berry), 33 (Steve
Lipofsky), 38 (Tim Pannell), 40 (Monica M. Davey/
epa), 41 (Matthew Roberts/Reuters), 42 (Ashley
Cooper), 45 (Sandro di Carlo Darsa/PhotoAlto), 47
(Maria Marogianni/PAP), 51 (Darren Whiteside/
Reuters); Getty Images pp 11 (Clive Rose), 18 (AFP), 19
(Mat Szwajkos/Stringer), 30 (Kevin Winter), 31 (Chris
Hondros), 34 (Andrew H. Walker); iStockphoto pp 8
(Pavel Losevsky), 14 (Sarah Hipwell), 17 (Alija), 25
(Leontura), 39 (Robert Pears), 48 (Richard Bowden), 50
(Kai Chiang); Shutterstock pp 4 (Junial Enterprises),
6 (loriklaszlo), 7 (Galina Barskaya), 9 (hurricane),
10 (Darren Green), 12 (© Golden Pixels LLC), 15
(Catalin Petolea), 23 (oliveromg), 26 (Morgan Lane
Photography), 36 (Ronald Caswell).

Cover photograph of a brother and sister reading a book
together on a porch swing, reproduced with permission
of Masterfile.

Every effort has been made to contact copyright holders
of material reproduced in this book. Any omissions will
be rectified in subsequent printings if notice is given to
the publisher.

Disclaimer
All the internet addresses (URLs) given in this book
were valid at the time of going to press. However, due to
the dynamic nature of the internet, some addresses may
have changed, or sites may have changed or ceased to
exist since publication. While the author and publisher
regret any inconvenience this may cause readers, no
responsibility for any such changes can be accepted by
either the author or the publisher.

Contents

In order to protect the privacy of individuals featured in case studies, some names have been changed.

Words appearing in the text in bold, **like this**, are explained in the Glossary.

What makes a hero?

Who is your idea of a hero? A comic-strip character with superpowers, or your favourite footballer or movie star? What about political leaders, scientists, and soldiers?

Perhaps you think that only extraordinary people can become heroes. You might be amazed to learn that you could be a hero yourself. Yes – YOU! Do you want to unlock your own secret powers? Then read on...

If you look out for people who are younger than you, then you could be a hero.

Heroes are all around us. They could be:

- soldiers in the military
- nurses and doctors
- charity workers
- explorers
- your teacher
- your older sister (who always helps you with your maths homework).

Can you think of any more heroes to add to the list?

listen up!

Quiz

Could you be a hero?

1. Your younger brother is being bullied at school. Do you:
   a. tell your brother not to be a wimp
   b. glare at the bullies but do nothing
   c. spend time listening to your brother and persuade him that he should tell his teacher.

2. There's a new kid in your class who has moved from another country. Do you:
   a. steer clear of her because you only hang out with people like yourself
   b. speak to her in class but that's it
   c. make an effort to talk to her, and invite her to join in with you and your friends.

3. You're hanging out with your friends in the street when an older neighbour asks you to keep the noise down. Do you:
   a. shout rudely at him, or ignore him
   b. move down the street but carry on making a noise
   c. apologize and try to be quieter.

Find out the truth!

If your answers were:

Mostly a's: you probably could do great things, but at the moment you're not giving yourself a chance. Read this book to find out ways to be a hero.

Mostly b's: you keep your head down when you should be sticking your neck out! Read this book to get more confident at doing the right thing. Learn how to release your inner hero!

Mostly c's: you're already showing signs of being a hero. Read this book to find some new and challenging ways to do the right thing.

Being a friend

Our relationships with our friends and family can be the most important in our lives. We rely on them to help us deal with problems, and we can enjoy chatting and laughing with them. Friends and family can give us the confidence we need to do well. But it's a two-way street. We need to be careful to give back as much as we take.

What can you do to be a good friend and help your family? Check out this section to see how a real hero is a great friend.

Best friends are people who make each other feel great.

01 Always be ready to listen. If a friend needs to talk about something, be there for them without butting in to talk about yourself.

02 Trust matters. If a friend tells you a secret, it means they trust you. Show them they were right to do so by keeping the secret, even if you're dying to tell it to other people.

> **"I have absolutely infinite respect for my mum and dad and my best friend, Will, whom I've known since I was 12. They're sort of my main influences in my life really."**
>
> Daniel Radcliffe, actor

Don't get hung up on wanting everyone to like you. Life's not like that. We all get on better with some people than we do with others. If you know that someone doesn't want to be your friend, just let it go. Focus on the people who do like your company.

03 Don't think you have to agree with your friends on everything. If they have different ideas or want to do an activity you dislike, that's fine. Just do your own thing until you're all ready to be together again.

04 The best thing about friendship is having a laugh. Enjoy joking around with your mates. But remember there are times when you should take them seriously, too.

05 Try to show that you're pleased when a friend has a bit of good luck, or does particularly well at something. Don't spoil his or her enjoyment by showing that you're envious, or complaining that it's "not fair".

06 Equally, if it's *you* who has done well or had a lucky break, try not to boast. Instead, if you can, share your luck with your friends.

07 Keeping secrets matters. But if a friend is doing something risky or dangerous, always talk to them about it. If you are really worried, talk to an adult you trust. Your friend's safety is more important than a secret.

Always make time to talk to a friend if you are worried about them.

Making friends

Not everyone finds it easy to make and keep new friends. Even the most popular people have to work at this. Here are some tips on how to be a mate magnet:

08 You have to be in the right place to make friends. It's no good sitting at home in front of a screen. Get out and be with other people.

09 Be friendly to everyone, not just your mates. There could be some really cool people around you if you just get to know them! You're more likely to make friends if you are a fun and open person to everyone.

10 Never bully or laugh at other people. If someone isn't your type, just let them be.

11 When you meet someone new, ask them questions about themselves. Don't just chatter on about yourself!

12 Don't gossip about other people. If you spread nasty rumours you might end up losing friends rather than gaining new ones. Nobody will trust you not to say the same about them.

It's not nice to feel left out. If you see someone on their own, you could ask them to join you and your friends.

Green-eyed monster alert!

Hannah and Carly had been best friends forever. Hannah thought Carly was the funniest, kindest, most all-round amazing person on the planet. But last summer Hannah started to hate hanging around with Carly. How come?

Answer: because Carly had met a new friend, Jaimee, at her dance class and they had become very close. Carly wanted Jaimee to join her and Hannah when they went to the beach or the park. But Hannah didn't like sharing her friend and started making excuses to stay at home. Carly didn't understand why, and thought Hannah just didn't like her any more. In the end they were hardly speaking to each other.

Then, one day Carly went to Hannah's house and refused to leave until Hannah told her what the problem was. When Hannah told Carly she was jealous of Jaimee, Carly listened and gave her friend a hug. She explained they would never stop being friends but that didn't mean they couldn't have other friends, too. Hannah gave Jaimee a chance and found out she liked her! She also started spending time with other friends from school as well as Carly.

And the moral is ... Just because you are best friends with someone it doesn't mean you can't have other friends. Don't hold each other back and you'll enjoy the time you spend together so much more.

Mouth open, brain in reverse?

Did you put your foot in your mouth? Have you fallen out with your best mate? Here are some ideas to help you patch things up:

13 Your friend played really badly in a team sport – and you told them so.
- DON'T say, "OK, I'm sorry I said that, BUT..." and then make things worse by piling on more criticism.
- DO say, "I'm really, really sorry I said that. The whole team needs to try harder. Please forgive me."

14 A good friend has criticized you for the way you did something.
- DON'T say, "You're an idiot and I don't want to speak to you ever again."
- DO say, "Ouch! That hurt! But I guess you could have a point. I'll think it over."

15 You find out a friend has lied to you.
- DON'T sulk and avoid them.
- DO say, "I don't know why you lied to me. But I still want to be your friend so please don't do it again." (Unless it's a really BIG lie.)

16 Whatever you have argued about, try to be the first to say sorry. Your friendship is more important than any stupid fight.

It can be hard to admit you were in the wrong, but it is better to apologize than risk falling out with your friends.

Hero profile

Name: Tom Daley
Date of birth: 21 May 1994
Nationality: British
Claim to fame: World Diving Champion at the age of 15
Badge of courage: youngest finalist at the 2008 Olympic Games, gold medallist at the 2009 World Championship, and double gold medallist at the 2010 Commonwealth Games.

After 14-year-old Tom competed at the 2008 Olympics, he had to go back to school and try to lead a normal life, despite being famous around the world. Perhaps other kids at his school were jealous, because he was badly bullied.

It reached the point where Tom couldn't go outside at break time because one bully had threatened to break his legs. He relied on four good friends who stuck with him through the bullying. Eventually Tom was lucky enough to move to another school.

Tom hasn't forgotten his experience – or the friends who helped him through it. They were his heroes. He now works with the children's helpline ChildLine, supporting young people who are suffering bullying and other problems.

Peter Bradley from the charity Kidscape says, "Tom was brave in telling others he was having trouble ... We hope that all young people will realize that the first step to breaking the chain of bullying is asking for help, and refusing to let the bullies win."

Respect

You may have heard people talking about respect. But what exactly does it mean? Some people seem to think it means making others do what they want. But respect is a two-way process. We all deserve respect from others, but *only* if we show it back to them. Here are some top tips on keeping the respect going around.

17 Respect is all about treating others as you'd like them to treat you. Try to think about what you are doing or saying to someone and ask yourself if you'd like to be treated that way.

18 Respect your friends' right to say "no", and don't try to push them into doing things they don't want to do. Remember, they have as much right to their opinions and choices as you do.

19 Always stay calm, even if you think someone has misjudged you. If you can explain your point of view quietly and politely, you might change people's minds.

Always think about other people's feelings when you talk to them.

20 Respecting your teachers doesn't mean that you have to be a grovelling teacher's pet. Teachers are trying to do a job that will ultimately help you. Anything you can do, such as listening quietly or doing your homework on time, will help them in return. You will make them respect you, too.

21 Young people often get a bad press on television and in newspapers. As a result, many older people think most kids are badly behaved. Show them they're wrong by being polite and respectful when you're out and about.

22 It's not just older people that you should show respect to. You should respect everyone, whether they are your age or younger than you.

Show respect by noticing what the people around you need.

"I'm not concerned with your liking or disliking me . . . All I ask is that you respect me as a human being."

Jackie Robinson, baseball player and political activist

Respecting yourself

23 If you make an occasional mistake and do something that makes you lose some of your self-respect, don't worry. Everyone makes mistakes. Try to learn from what went wrong.

24 Never be a bully, or poke fun at people who are shy, or have some sort of disability. It may seem hilarious to you and your friends at the time, but it's an unkind and disrespectful way to behave. You will not respect yourself for it in later life.

25 You only get one body! Show it some respect by taking care of it. Try to eat healthy food, keep active, and get enough rest.

26 *Think* before sending that text message or email! Have you said anything you might later regret? Always watch what you write because it could come back to haunt you. (And remember that anything you put on the internet is probably there to stay.)

> **"They cannot take away our self-respect if we do not give it to them."**
>
> Mahatma Gandhi, political and spiritual leader

Take time to consider the other person's feelings before you send a text message.

We all know what it's like to feel bad about something we have done. Try to learn from the experience and move on.

Think before you do it!

Caris has learned a lot about self-respect lately. Her friends were joking around with mobile phones and daring each other to take silly photos. Caris thought it was a laugh to join in. But the next thing she knew, there were embarrassing pictures of her on the internet and everyone in her class was laughing at her. Worse than that, some people were calling her names or stopped talking to her.

Caris was upset that she had let herself down. She told her family and they told her to put it behind her. Her real friends have stuck with her and Caris has learned never to lose her dignity again.

And the moral is ... Always think about your own self-respect when you take photos or post things on the internet. You have no idea who might see these things. Make sure you are happy for anyone to look at them, including your family.

Quiz

True or false?

a) If an adult asks you to stop doing something, they are not showing you respect.

b) You don't need to show respect for people you don't like.

c) Whatever you have done in the past, you can always have self-respect.

d) To be a good friend, you need to show respect.

Find out the truth!

a. False. You might be doing something that upsets other people or that might be dangerous to you. Unless they are rude to you, try to listen to them politely and consider their point of view so they see you can show respect yourself.

b. False. We can't all like everybody, and we are all different. We need to respect this and be polite to everyone if we want them to show us respect in return.

c. True. So long as you learn from your mistakes and promise yourself NEVER to make them again, you can always start over.

d. True. We need to respect everyone, even our closest friends. Just because you are close to someone it doesn't mean you can take them for granted. Remember to treat them in the way you'd like them to treat you.

Respecting your surroundings

As well as other people, we should show respect for the world around us. This includes other people's belongings, and the planet we live on.

27 How would you feel if a football smashed through your living room window? Shocked? Angry? When you're out with friends, think about what you're doing. Are you just having fun or could you be damaging something that belongs to someone else?

28 You've finished your sandwich but there isn't a rubbish bin by your elbow to dump the empty wrapper. Don't be a SLOB and drop it on the ground! Carry your rubbish with you until you find a bin.

29 When you leave a fast food restaurant do you leave your empty cartons and cups on the table? You could make things easier for the people who work there by clearing away your rubbish. After all, it could be YOU working in that restaurant one day!

30 Leaving lights, televisions, and computers switched on and zapping up energy in an empty room is not very clever. Remember to switch off all electrical appliances when you're not using them.

31 Don't waste water or food. Try to recycle whenever you can instead of just binning your rubbish.

32 Join an organization that campaigns for the environment. It could be to do with any issue that interests you, such as wildlife or saving energy.

Recycling is an easy way to show respect for the planet.

Simple solutions

Celebrities are not the only "green" heroes out there. Many ordinary people are finding ways to respect the planet by doing simple things that save energy and reduce pollution. Remember, we *all* need to start making changes for the good of the whole world.

33 Reuse or repair something instead of binning it.

34 Borrow something instead of buying new stuff – or consider buying used items. Charity shops are great sources of cool vintage chic!

35 Recycling includes buying recycled items. Look out for products made from recycled materials.

listen up!

Want some inspiration on how to show the planet real respect? Many famous people are taking the lead and showing us how it's possible to have a busy, exciting lifestyle and still think about the environment.

Leonardo DiCaprio walks the green walk and talks the green talk. He avoids the private jets that many celebrities use, and drives an environmentally friendly car. He's made films to inform people about the environment and has started his own organization to support causes he believes in.

36 Recycle empty glass bottles and jars. The energy saved by recycling one bottle can power a computer for 25 minutes.

37 Make sure your taps are turned off. A dripping tap could waste up to 5,000 litres (1,100 gallons) of water in one year.

38 Donate the clothes, electronics, toys, and other things you no longer use to a charity shop or local school instead of adding them to **landfill sites**.

What's that?

A **landfill site** is a large expanse of land where litter and waste are buried.

Cameron Diaz shows respect for the environment. She recycles and drives a carbon-friendly car. She has also become involved in the former US Vice President Al Gore's campaign to raise awareness about climate change.

Cameron says, "If everyone just changed one aspect of their life, if they just did one thing differently, that alone is a step closer to solving the problem. This problem can be solved."

These stars realize that by making the effort to "green-up" their own lifestyles, they can act as role models to millions of people.

Taking the lead

At some point in your life, you may be asked to take the lead in a particular situation. For example, you could be asked to head up a school committee for a fun run, or find yourself promoted to captain of a sports team.

Knowing that you have the responsibility of leading others (and for raising loads of money, or helping to train up a brilliant team) can be super-scary. But it's also a great way to find out how to get the best out of other people, and yourself.

So, do you have the makings of a leader? What makes a good leader? Read on to find out.

Prime ministers and presidents such as Barack Obama aren't the only leaders. You can be one, too!

> "Change will not come if we wait for some other person or some other time. We are the ones we've been waiting for. We are the change that we seek."

Barack Obama, US President

BE SMART

Nothing ventured, nothing gained!

"Well, I've often thought I'd *like* to volunteer to lead something, but I know I'd be rubbish at it..." Hmm – sound familiar? Unless you give it a try, you'll never know whether you're rubbish or not! Start by picking a small project. You might surprise yourself.

39 Good leaders are good listeners – they don't boss people around. Always make time to hear everyone's opinions. Let them know that their thoughts and feelings matter.

40 Good leaders are honest. Don't pretend to be anything you're not. Be straight with people from the start, and they'll be clear about what you can and can't do.

41 Good leaders are firm but fair. If others criticize what you are doing, listen to what they're saying. Do they have a valid point? If you're sure that they don't, and that they're just making trouble for the sake of it, tell them to either help out or back out.

42 Try not to take on more than you and your team can realistically handle. For example, your school dance committee might have the time and money to organize a fab firework display to end the evening. But you might be stretching your resources if you *also* try to have a cool, suspended LED dance platform...

Quiz

Can you hold out against peer pressure?

1. One boy in your class is picked on and teased by everyone else. You:
   - a. join in and laugh at him, too
   - b. just ignore it
   - c. talk to him and encourage your friends to do the same.

2. Your friends are doing something that's against the law and could be dangerous. You:
   - a. go along with them and hope that you don't get caught
   - b. make an excuse so you don't have to join in
   - c. talk to them about why taking this risk is a seriously bad idea.

3. You're interested in joining a new club but your friends laugh at you and say it sounds boring. You:
   - a. decide not to join the club and hang out with your friends instead
   - b. join the club but don't tell anyone about it
   - c. get active in the new club and explain to your friends why you like it.

Find out the truth!

If your answers were:

Mostly a's: You worry too much about what other people think. Other people seem to be making your choices for you. Try to be more assertive and stand up for what you want to do.

Mostly b's: You don't like to rock the boat but you know when it's a bad idea to follow the crowd. You've done well not to get pressured into doing things you don't want, but why not try to take the lead and show other people another way to go?

Mostly c's: You're strong enough to stand up to peer pressure and go your own way. It's not always easy though, is it? Read on to learn about some ways to make taking the lead a little less stressful.

Holding your ground

It can often feel really hard to say "no" to something you just don't want to do - and keep your friends. Here are some top tips on how to hold your ground.

43 Stay calm and relaxed. If others are trying to persuade you to do something and you become angry or stressed, they probably won't give up bugging you.

44 If friends put pressure on you to do something that you don't want to do, tell them it's their choice and that's fine, but you're making another choice. Be polite, and then just walk away.

45 Don't worry about missing out if you don't follow the crowd. There'll always be others who agree with you. You'd only feel bad afterwards if you did something that didn't feel right for you.

46 If you think a group of friends are about to do something stupid, try suggesting something else to do. They might just be bored and may welcome another idea.

47 Another way to stop friends pushing you into doing stuff you don't want to do is to ask them WHY they want you to do it. They might find this hard to explain if they think about it.

Take time to think about what *you* want to do before you follow your friends.

What other qualities do good leaders need?

Don't leaders have to be loud and bossy?

No! A good leader needs to listen to others as well as communicate. The best leaders speak to others clearly and calmly and make sure they get plenty of other people involved. It's not just about telling other people what to do.

Only popular people can be leaders, right?

Think about the people you know who are "popular". They are probably the ones who try the hardest to fit in with the crowd. They're not always the ones who make good leaders. A good leader might have to make decisions that some people don't like. They have to include and get on with everyone, not just the cool crowd.

I feel shy in a big group so I could never be a leader, could I?

You might be a very good leader. Try taking the lead in a small group first, for example in class. Think about what you are good at. Perhaps you're a good listener or you are good at helping a group make decisions. These are all great leadership skills. Remember what your strengths are and perhaps you'll be confident enough to take the lead with a larger group next time.

Oops!

It's not all plain sailing when you take the lead. But don't let that put you off. You'll learn from your own mistakes. Here are some tips to start you off:

48 You've lost it with a group who can't make a decision and you yelled at them.
DON'T say: "You're all useless, I'll make the decision myself!"
DO say something like, "I'm sorry I lost my cool. This is a tough decision to make, isn't it? Let's write a list of pros and cons together."

49 You're finding it hard to get other people to help with an activity.
DON'T just do it yourself because it's easier than persuading others to help.
DO talk to people one at a time and see what small tasks they can each take on.

50 There is a lot of work to be done and you're leading an enthusiastic team.
DON'T sit back and let them do all the work.
DO pitch in and try to get involved a little in what everyone is doing.

51 DON'T expect everyone to be your friend when you are the leader.
DO respect them and expect them to respect you in return.

52 DON'T just assume everyone is happy and everything is going to plan.
DO keep talking to everyone and make sure they let you know if there are any problems so you can deal with them fast.

A good leader makes sure everybody feels included.

I took the lead!

Saeed and his class thought they were pretty eco-aware. At home they switched off lights and recycled paper and packaging. But Saeed couldn't understand why so much rubbish from the school canteen just ended up in the bins.

"Nobody seemed to have noticed that all this packaging was just going off to landfill sites when so much of it could have been recycled. So I decided to do something about it."

Saeed held a meeting with other pupils to talk about what they could do to solve the problem. He spoke to the head teacher and arranged for recycling bins to be provided in the canteen. Then Saeed organized a group that went round all the classes in the school to talk to pupils about separating rubbish and putting it in the proper bins. The group also made posters reminding everyone to use the bins.

Saeed was really pleased with the results. "Everyone could see the idea made sense. We even started composting some of the food waste and it's used to grow vegetables in the school grounds. Now our group is looking at recycling in our town and trying to persuade more people to get involved."

And the moral is ... We can all make a difference. Don't wait for someone else to take the lead if you can get things started yourself.

When other people see you doing the right thing, they will often join in.

26

Every member of a team has to take the lead sometimes.

Taking a sporting lead

Leading a sports team can be challenging and sometimes frustrating! Here are some tips on how to get the best results from your teammates:

53 Encourage your teammates! Some of them might not be feeling very confident, but if you make them feel supported they'll play much better.

54 Always respect the referee or umpire's decisions. Try not lose your cool even if you don't agree. (Take note: the football stars you see arguing with the ref on television never get their own way!)

55 Take the lead by respecting the rules. Rules are there so that everyone can enjoy the game safely. Cheating or fouling just holds the game up.

56 A true hero respects his or her opponents, even if they win. And when *you* win, try to treat your opponents well, too.

What is a role model?

While you're growing up, there's usually somebody out there who makes you think, "*That's* what I want to be like!" This person may live or behave in a certain way or believe in things that you also think are important. Whatever the case, this person becomes your role model.

Perhaps a parent or other relative is your role model? Or a coach, or a teacher? For many people today, their heroes and role models are famous people – the sports stars, singers, and actors who we see on our screens and read about in magazines.

Read on to find out more about role models – and how they can be good for us, or turn bad.

listen up!

What do you think makes someone a good role model? You could try making a mental list of the sorts of personal qualities you admire, and that you'd like to develop in yourself. These might include:

- kindness
- generosity
- intelligence
- sense of humour
- self-discipline
- truthfulness
- modesty
- loyalty
- courage

Does your current hero or role model have any of the qualities on your list?

Learn from mistakes

Sometimes stars let fame go to their heads and act in disrespectful or unhealthy ways. Try to learn from their mistakes. But other stars see fame as an opportunity to do the right thing, knowing that many people are watching what they do. Look out for the celebrities who are showing respect for themselves and others.

Marion Jones made the wrong choice when she took drugs to help her win races.

Oops!

How does it affect you when famous people let themselves and everyone else down?

- How do you feel when you discover that an athlete you admire took drugs to win an important race? Running superstars such as Justin Gatlin, Marion Jones, and Dwain Chambers not only let fans down by taking drugs, they also gave their sport a bad name. Sometimes a role model's actions can affect many other people, not just themselves.

- What message do you get when famous footballers shout at the referee, or attack other players during a match? That this is a cool way to be? Er – no and no! There's never an excuse for "foul" behaviour, on or off the pitch. (And it's *so* NOT cool to wreck your own World Cup dreams and disappoint your fans by getting sent off mid-match.)

But perhaps stars who are bad role models can teach us things, too – such as, how *not* to behave?

Quiz

Is your celebrity hero a good role model?

1. Good role models lead a healthy lifestyle. Does your hero look after him or herself? Yes/No

2. Good role models are respectful. They look out for their friends and support others less well off than themselves. Does your hero respect other people? Yes/No

3. A good role model keeps a balance in their life. Does your hero manage to work hard but also spend time relaxing with family and friends? Yes/No

4. A good role model can remain calm and polite even when under pressure. Does you hero keep his or her cool even when photographers follow him or her everywhere? Yes/No

5. Does your hero recognize that he or she might be a role model to people like you? Do you think he or she cares what you think of them? Yes/No

Find out the truth!

If you answered mostly "yes," then your celebrity hero really is a good role model. But don't be disappointed if they sometimes make mistakes – we're all human!

If you answered mostly "no," then you might want to ask yourself why this person is your hero. Have they changed since they became famous? Try not to copy some of their bad choices and think about other stars who might be better role models.

Here are some stars who set a fantastic example to all their fans:

- *Harry Potter* star Emma Watson knows how to take care of herself and her body. Despite her fame and wealth, she decided to finish her university education. She also makes hockey and tennis a regular part of her life. Emma says, "Sport really makes me feel good about myself."

- Both fans and tennis opponents like and respect Spanish tennis superstar Rafael Nadal, for his willingness to sign autographs and his **graciousness** in defeat. He has even said, "You need a defeat to give value to your victories."

- US basketball legend Shaquille O'Neal made sure he finished his education even though he'd already made his fortune on the basketball court. He manages to fit in a career as a rap singer and as a reserve police officer while spending plenty of time with his family.

Shaquille O'Neal has shown his kids that getting an education is as important as money or fame.

Looking below the surface

62 It's very easy to admire, or even hero-worship, someone just because they are SERIOUSLY good-looking! But what's going on inside this person? Do you admire their character, as well as their face and figure? Always try to ask yourself these questions before you choose a beautiful role model.

63 Another downside to choosing beautiful role models is fairly obvious: you may feel you could never look as good as they do! This can be really bad for your **self esteem**, and even make you feel depressed. Try to choose role models who show you how you could *be*, rather than how you could look.

What's that?

Your **self esteem** is the way you see yourself. It can be a positive, or negative view.

Hero profile

Name: Aimee Mullins
Date of birth: 1976
Nationality: American
Claim to fame: athlete, model, and actress

Aimee Mullins lost both of her legs below the knee when she was only one year old. But she grew up joining in with all the other kids, playing sports and having fun. Aimee excelled at school and went on to be an athlete, running in the Paralympic Games in Atlanta in 1996. She held world records in the 100 metres, 200 metres, and long jump. She has also worked in the body-conscious worlds of modelling and acting.

Aimee says that having confidence is much more important than what you look like. She now spends time speaking to people about positive body image and making sports available to everyone.

64 Do you sometimes back off from people who you think are "weird" in some way? They may look unfashionable or "geeky", or they could even have a disability. Remember, these people may have qualities you wish you had. Try to find out by giving them a chance.

Are you a role model?

You yourself might already be a role model for younger children around you. Here are some top tips on how to set a great example:

65 Try to be respectful with younger kids and listen to their opinions. If you think they've got it wrong, don't just shout at them and tell them they're "stupid". Ask them why they think like that. Then suggest some other ways of thinking. Have a discussion, not an argument.

66 Don't tease younger children in front of other people so that they feel **humiliated**. Remember, you were a little kid, too, not so long ago! You'd have *hated* that, wouldn't you?

What's that?

To **humiliate** someone means to make them feel ashamed and uncomfortable – usually in public.

67 If you see that a younger child is frightened of doing something, try to help them overcome their fear. If possible, do it with them until they feel confident enough to try on their own.

68 Try to be patient with younger children and understand their point of view. They don't have your knowledge or experience of the world. They may feel insecure, or misunderstand what is expected of them.

Everyday heroes

Some of the best role models are not famous at all! Ordinary people can still be heroes, even if they're not known all over the world or earning millions.

Look around you and you'll see all sorts of incredible people out there who are fighting against problems or being brave every day. Some are standing up for what they believe in; others are just doing their jobs to keep the rest of us safe. There are the people who rescue us from fires, or keep us alive after accidents. There are also people who give their time to support others in their local community.

These are the real heroes – and they come in all ages and sizes. You could even be one yourself!

Firefighters sometimes risk their own lives to help others.

Firefighters, paramedics, lifeboat crews, mountain rescue teams, and police officers – all of these people take risks and work hard to keep the rest of us safe. Find out more about the work they do. (If you also listen to their advice you will be helping them, too.)

listen up!

Could you be a local hero?

Maybe you'd love to be out there helping in some way – but you don't quite know how to begin? Check out these ideas and unleash the hero in yourself!

69 Take a look in your local paper or watch your local news. These are good places to spot heroes who have done something (even something simple) to help other people. They could inspire you.

70 Think about your family. Does your mum, dad, sister, or brother give some of his or her time to help others? Talk to them about what they do. Would this be something you'd like to do, too?

71 Are there things at school that could be changed for the better? Consider joining your school council so that you are in a good position to make things happen.

72 Look at your local community. Is enough being done to help young people, old people, animals, or the environment? If not, perhaps you and your friends could do something about it.

"My heroes are and were my parents. I can't see having anyone else as my heroes."

Michael Jordan

Kids can make a difference

Heroes can be any age. Here are the true stories of some courageous and determined kids to inspire you:

- William is only seven years old, but while other kids his age are out playing and having fun, he is helping to look after his mum. She has a disease called **multiple sclerosis**, and William often has to help her with every day activities, or call for help when she needs it. His mum says, "If it wasn't for William I might not be here today."

- Courtney was 10 years old when she saved her family from a fire in their home. She'd learned what to do at school so she put a damp towel at the bottom of the door to stop smoke getting into the room, and told everyone to lie on the floor. Then she climbed out of a window and ran down the road for help.

- Tara was 14 when she saw that the teenagers where she lived had nothing to do. She set up a club where kids can go and keep off the streets. She and other teenagers design and sell T-shirts to raise money for the club.

And the moral is ... Anyone can be a hero! It doesn't matter how old you are or where you live. Do you know any kids who deserve to be called heroes?

What's that?

Multiple sclerosis is a disease of the nervous system that causes weakness of the muscles, and loss of movement. There is no known cure.

These young volunteers are helping to build homes in their community.

If you learn First Aid you could save someone's life.

You can be an everyday hero just by learning a few simple skills. Just one of these could help you to help someone else – and perhaps even save a life.

73 Anyone can learn First Aid. Even if you just know the basics you could stop an injury becoming serious. You might keep someone alive until the paramedics arrive. Find out about First Aid courses in your school or community.

74 Are you a good swimmer? Maybe you could train as a lifeguard. If you learn lifesaving skills you could help other people and it might be a good holiday job when you are older.

75 Visit your local fire station and get all the info on house fires. Your knowledge could prevent a fire happening in your house, but if you do find yourself in one then you'll know what to do.

76 Listening is a simple skill, but it's so important. If friends know they can trust you to listen and support them then you might be able to help them deal with all kinds of problems.

77 Do you already have a special skill that could help raise money for charity? Your skill could be mending bikes, woodworking, or even face-painting. Don't be shy – just put yourself forward!

Ordinary heroes hit the headlines

Here are some stories about ordinary heroes who hit the headlines for their bravery and **selflessness**:

Hero profile: the Hudson River hero

On 15th January 2009, US Airways Flight 1549 took off from New York City. As the passenger plane flew upwards, a flock of geese hit it and damaged both engines. The pilot, Chesley "Sully" Sullenberger, knew he had to land the plane fast but there was no time to get to an airport. Even worse, he was flying over a busy city! Sully decided to use the Hudson River as a runway. He kept his cool and managed to land the plane safely in the water. Incredibly, the crew and passengers all survived.

Hero profile: hijack hero

If you think pirates only exist at the movies, you're wrong! In 2009, Captain Richard Phillips ran into danger when pirates invaded and hijacked his cargo ship near the East African coast. Captain Phillips gave himself up as a hostage to protect his crew. He was finally rescued by the US Navy, and praised by the US President for risking his own life to save his crew.

Hero profile: sea rescue hero

Samantha Davies is another hero of the sea. This British sailor came third in a round-the-world sailing race in 2009. Not only did she manage this all on her own but during the race she had to go on a rescue mission. Another competitor had broken his leg so Sam sailed to help him, perhaps giving up her chance of winning the race.

What's that?

Selflessness means thinking of others before yourself.

Hero profile: cancer hero

In 2000, British woman Jane Tomlinson discovered she was suffering from cancer and would not recover. She decided to spend the time she had left

raising money for charity. Over the next 6 years she ran 4 marathons, took part in 2 triathlons, and cycled across the United States, Europe, and Africa. She once said, "I feel I've done more than a lot of people do in a lifetime." By the time she died in 2007, Jane had raised £1.75 million for charity and encouraged many other people to start exercising.

Heroes who help

OK, so you might not have the skills to land a passenger plane in a river or negotiate with pirates, but that doesn't mean you can't be a hero.

Still not sure how you could make a difference? Why not think about being a volunteer. Giving your time and energy to projects you care about is a great feeling and it can change your life, too.

Read on for some ideas to get you started.

Giving to charities is a great way to help others.

78 Litter is a menace! It not only looks awful, it can seriously harm wildlife and the environment. You can start your own war on litter by always remembering to put your rubbish in a bin, or recycling it.

79 Studies have shown that people are less likely to drop litter in places that are clean and tidy. So even picking up a bit of litter in a public place can make a difference. Why not organize a group of friends for a "litter-blitz" and make your local community a litter-free zone?

80 Are you an animal lover? Go to your local animal shelter with an adult and see what you can do to help out. Is there an organization in your neighbourhood that looks after local wildlife and birds? See if you can help them out by looking after **habitats** or counting the number of birds that visit.

What's that?
A **habitat** is the area where an animal or plant normally lives or grows.

81 Make sure there's a company that collects your school's recycling. If there isn't, talk with your teacher. Maybe arranging for collection of your school's recyclables would be a good class project!

82 Remind others about what they can do to help the environment. Why not make some simple posters to put up around your school, community centre, or youth club? If people see a poster asking them "Have you switched off your computer?" they might remember to do it next time!

"If you ever need a helping hand, it is at the end of your arm. As you get older you must remember you have a second hand. The first one is to help yourself. The second hand is to help others."

Audrey Hepburn, actress

Why volunteer?

Still think volunteering is for other people? The first step is to think about what you are good at, or interested in. Then find out if there's a chance for you to volunteer in that area. You could even start your own group to make a change.

Volunteering helps everyone

case study

Tyrone was getting bored over the long summer holiday so he decided to volunteer at a summer camp for disabled kids. He started out thinking it would just be a way to pass the time and help him get a place at uni. He didn't realise how much fun it would be. He's already signed up for next summer and is training to do more activities with disabled children.

Yasmin volunteers at a city farm near her home. She's always loved animals and this gives her a chance to look after many different types! It's good physical work so she's feeling much fitter and has made some great new friends.

Ash and his friends used their hip-hop dance skills to set up a theatre group. They've now got funding to visit several cities so they can perform for kids and warn them about gangs.

And the moral is ... Volunteering can be a way to help yourself as well as others.

Are you a people person?

If you love to be around people, here are some ideas for ways to help out in your local community:

83 Help older people! If you have older relations or neighbours, you could offer to tidy up their gardens or fetch shopping.

84 Do you know of any lonely people in your neighbourhood? They may have been recently widowed, or their family lives far away, or perhaps they've recently moved to the area and don't know anyone nearby? Take time to chat to them when you get the opportunity.

85 Take dogs for walks! You may know people who find it hard to make time to take their dog out for a long walk. You could help out and get fit at the same time.

86 You're reading this book – aren't you lucky? There may be younger children you know who need help learning to read. Offer to listen to them read and make sure you tell them when they are doing well.

87 Organize a team sports activity or fun run at your school to raise money for charity and get everyone active.

If everybody helps a little then big change can happen.

BE SMART

Make sure you tell your parents or guardians before you offer help in your neighbourhood. They will want to know where you are at all times and to make sure that you will be safe. Also, if you are younger than 13 years old, you should not offer yourself as a dog walker.

Heroes in adversity

Sometimes people become heroes through overcoming **adversity** (bad luck or tragedy). While battling with difficult situations, they discover courage and strength they never knew they had.

On these pages you will read about some heroes who wouldn't let any problems stand in the way of what they wanted to achieve. Often their tough experiences have inspired them to help others, too.

"When fate hands us a lemon, let's try to make a lemonade."

Dale Carnegie, author

Hero profile: running for gold!

Kenyan paralympic athlete Henry Kirwa was born with visual disabilities. His family lived in an area of Kenya where disabled children were hidden away, so he was not expected to do much with his life. But Henry had other ideas. "I decided on running ... However friends and neighbours brushed off my dreams and suggested that I ... got down to tilling land."

But Henry trained hard at his running, and in 2008 he won three gold medals at the Beijing Paralympic Games. In 2009, he was named United Nations Person of the Year in Kenya. Henry has become a hero and inspiration to many young, disabled Africans. He is now active in persuading Kenyan families to stop hiding their disabled children and instead help them develop their talents.

Hero profile: *Atlantic victory*

Twelve British and American ex-servicemen became the first ever all-**amputee** sailing crew to race across the Atlantic Ocean in 2008. Most had lost a limb fighting in Iraq or Afghanistan. One crew member, Captain Bernie Bambury, wrote this in his diary when they completed their journey: "We have shown, I believe, that disability … is not a barrier to achievement. Any barriers that may exist, exist only in people's minds."

Hero profile: *the Paradox Sports team*

The Paradox Sports team shows us that disabled people can take part in outdoor adventures and sports. They raise money to help make this happen, taking on challenges such as ice climbing, skydiving, kayaking, and mountain biking.

Paradox people include D. J. Skelton, who was wounded whilst serving as a soldier in Iraq, and Malcolm Daly, who lost a foot to frostbite in a climbing accident. Another team member says, "Most things that I've tried to do, I've been able to do. I just want to help other people do the same."

Ade Adepitan (left) had polio when he was a child. He went on to compete internationally in wheelchair basketball and to work as a presenter for the BBC. He has been awarded an MBE for his contributions to disabled sport.

Just be yourself

You don't have to face death or help millions of people to be a hero. Believe it or not, it's enough to just be yourself.

It's not always easy – how many times have you had to deal with people who want you to do something you know is a bad idea? Isn't it just easier to go along with what they want and stay popular? The trouble is, you never feel happy with yourself when that happens.

It takes bravery to be yourself and stick up for what you want and believe in. But you can do it. Read on to get some tips on how to get real.

Try to spend time with friends who let you be yourself.

> **"Always be a first-rate version of yourself, instead of a second-rate version of somebody else."**
>
> Judy Garland, actor and singer

88 Be curious. Find out about the world you live in and form your own opinions. Don't let other people tell you what to think.

89 If you think something is wrong, don't just moan about it. Think about what you could do to make positive changes.

90 Don't think the only friends worth having are the cool crowd. There are so many other people around you who could be great friends and will let you be yourself.

91 Stand up to bullying! If you see people getting picked on in your school, talk to your friends and teachers about ways to tackle the bullies.

92 Don't be afraid to move on from friends who don't let you be yourself. You don't have to fight – just start to spend more time with other people.

93 It can be hard if people don't like things about you. But we can't all be friends with everyone and there are probably things you don't like about them, too. Just try to focus on yourself and all your good points.

listen up!

How would you feel if you went outside and found the family car sprayed with graffiti? Or if you were driven mad all day and all night by the kid next door practising his drums? Remember the Golden Rule: behave towards others as you would like them to behave towards you. Don't make "being yourself" an excuse for bad or thoughtless behaviour.

I've had the same group of friends since I was small. Now they're all starting to smoke. I don't want to smoke but I don't want to feel left out. Don't I have to join in or I'll lose my friends?

Only you can make choices for yourself. Your friends might choose to do unhealthy (or even illegal) stuff, but if you don't want to join in, they should respect that. If they don't, then you might want to question why you are friends with them.

I'm not very interesting. People won't like me if I'm just myself, will they?

You're a much better friend if you're true to yourself than if you try to be someone else. But you don't have to change who you are to try new activities and make new friends. Everyone is interesting to someone out there so just get out there and try to believe in yourself.

There are plenty of people in your life who think you are interesting and fun to be with.

Rafael Nadal is a very successful tennis player. His passion and determination make him a role model for many of his fans.

94 It's fine to be competitive in a healthy way, but don't think you've *always* got to win or *always* have to be right. There will usually be people who know more about something, or are better at something than you. Try to learn from these people, and remember to praise them for their knowledge or skill.

95 Remember that younger kids look up to you. They might copy what you do and say. Do you want them to remember you as someone who helped them or someone who made them unhappy?

96 Try to lead a healthy lifestyle. Make the right choices and look after your body!

97 Always try your best. Don't worry about what everyone else is doing – if you know you have worked hard and done your best then you should be proud of yourself.

98 Always try to see the best in other people. You'll find they do the same for you in return.

99 Don't get too stressed when you make mistakes. Look at them as a fantastic learning opportunity!

100 You're responsible for yourself – nobody else is. So keep hold of your self-respect and dignity.

101 Believe that you *can* be a hero, and you *can* make a difference! Even the smallest actions can make change happen.

Glossary

adversity hardship or a difficult situation to overcome

amputee someone who has had part or all of a limb surgically removed

freeloader someone who takes advantage of the efforts or generosity of others, but contributes very little themselves

gracious being kind, respectful, and polite

habitat area where an animal or plant normally lives or grows

humiliate make someone feel ashamed and uncomfortable, usually in public

landfill site large expanse of land where man-made litter and waste are buried

multiple sclerosis disease of the nervous system that causes weakness of the muscles and loss of movement

self esteem describes how you see yourself. It can be a positive, or negative view.

selflessness thinking of others before yourself

Find out more

Books

21st Century Lives: Campaigners, Philip Steele (Wayland, 2009)

50 Simple Things You Can Do to Save the Earth, Jesse Javna, John Javna, and Sophie Javna (Hyperion, 2008)

Do the Right Thing: A Teenager's Survival Guide for Tricky Situations, Jane Goldman (Piccadilly Press, 2007)

Faces of Courage: Young Heroes of World War I, Sally M. Rogow (Granville Island Publishing, 2008)

Great Heroes: The Bill Gates Story – The Computer Genius Who Changed the World, Studio Cheongbi (Dasanbooks, 2009)

Heroes: A Guide to Realising Your Dreams, Jim Stynes, Paul Currie, John Carnegie (Allen & Unwin, 2005)

Independent Thinking: The Buzz - A Practical Confidence Builder for Teenagers, David Hodgson (Crown House Publishing, 2006)

Life Skills: Be Smart, Stay Safe!, Louise Spilsbury (Heinemann Library, 2009)

Life Skills: Get Green!, Anne Marie Todd (Heinemann Library, 2009)

Life Skills: Raising Money, Barbara Hollander (Heinemann Library, 2009)

Life Skills: Respect Others, Respect Yourself!, Sarah Medina (Heinemann Library, 2009)

Life Skills: Together as a Team!, Louise Spilsbury (Heinemann Library, 2009)

Making Healthy Food Choices: Food for Feeling Healthy, Carol Ballard (Heinemann Library, 2007)

Not Out: Heroes from the World of Sport, Nimish Dubey (Ponytail Books, 2010)

Out of Control: How to Handle Anger – Yours and Everyone Else's, John DiConsiglio (Children's Press, 2008)

The Girls' Book of Wisdom: Empowering, Inspirational Quotes from Over 400 Fabulous Females, Catherine Dee (Little Brown, 2008)

Women Heroes of World War II: 26 Stories of Espionage, Sabotage, Resistance, and Rescue, Kathryn J. Atwood (Chicago Review Press, 2011)

Websites

http://myhero.com/child/child_content.asp
Visit this website to read inspirational stories about child heroes.

www.childheroespublishing.com
Find books about children who are struggling with diseases, isolation, and other problems on this website.

www.foe.org.uk
Have a look at the Friends of the Earth website for ideas on how to get involved in campaigns to save the environment.

http://roycastle.org/kats
The website for Kids Against Tobacco Smoke offers help with quitting – or not starting in the first place!

www.teenagehealthfreak.org
This is a great website with advice and information on bullying, alcohol, drugs, moods, and much more.

www.disabled-world.com/artman/publish/famous-amputees.shtml
Find out about some well-known amputees (people who have had limbs removed) who have gone on to do great things with their lives.

Index